30-MINUTE OUTDOOR SCIENCE PROJECTS

Anna Leigh

Lerner Publications ◆ Minneapolis

Official Licensed Product
Lerner Publications Company
A division of Lerner Publishing Group, Inc.
241 First Avenue North
Minneapolis, MN 55401 USA

For reading levels and more information, look up this title at www.lernerbooks.com.

Main body text set in Hoosker Don't.
Typeface provided by The Chank Company.

Library of Congress Cataloging-in-Publication Data

Names: Leigh, Anna, author.
Title: 30-minute outdoor science projects / Anna Leigh.
Other titles: Thirty minute outdoor science projects
Description: Minneapolis : Lerner Publications, [2019] | Series: 30-minute makers |
    Audience: Ages 7–11. |
    Audience: Grades 4 to 6. | Includes bibliographical references and index.
Identifiers: LCCN 2018014512 (print) | LCCN 2018019035 (ebook) | ISBN
    9781541542907 (eb pdf)
    | ISBN 9781541538894 (lb : alk. paper)
Subjects: LCSH: Science—Experiments—Juvenile literature. | Science projects—
    Juvenile literature.
Classification: LCC Q182.3 (ebook) | LCC Q182.3 .L345 2019 (print) | DDC 507/.8—
    dc23
LC record available at https://lccn.loc.gov/2018014512

Manufactured in the United States of America
1-45072-35899-10/11/2018

CONTENTS

Think Outside the Box! – – – – – – – – 4

Before You Get Started – – – – – – – 6

Blowing Bubbles – – – – – – – – – 8

Homemade Compass – – – – – – – 10

Paper Airplanes – – – – – – – – 12

Kite Flight – – – – – – – – – – 15

Windy Weather – – – – – – – – 18

Heavy Hula – – – – – – – – – 20

Baking Soda Rocket – – – – – 22

Bug Vacuum – – – – – – – – 24

Take the Temperature – – – – 26

More to Explore – – – – – – 30

Glossary – – – – – – – – – 31

Further Information – – – – 31

Index – – – – – – – – – – 32

For even more
outdoor projects,
scan this QR code!

THINK OUTSIDE THE BOX!

What kind of science can you do in your own backyard? From blowing bubbles and launching rockets to measuring the wind and catching bugs, these fast, fun projects will help you explore the world, and maybe you'll even get a little messy while doing them!

When you finish each project, try making a few changes to see what happens. What scientific discoveries will you make outdoors?

BEFORE YOU GET STARTED

Many of these projects use materials that you can find around your home, such as paper, baking soda, cups, and bowls. Other materials should be easy to find at your local grocery store or hardware store.

Some projects use scissors or knives, and some require safety goggles. Make sure you always ask an adult for permission to do these projects and for help using sharp tools. Always wear your safety **goggles** when the instructions include them.

BLOWING BUBBLES

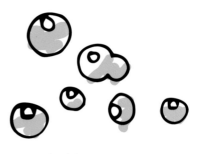

Make your own bubble wands and solution, and find out how to make the best bubbles!

🕐 **TIMEFRAME: 20~30 minutes**

MATERIALS

⇨ 3 pipe cleaners

⇨ permanent marker

⇨ masking tape

⇨ 3 large cups or bowls with wide openings

⇨ measuring cups

⇨ water

⇨ measuring spoons

⇨ liquid dishwashing soap

⇨ glycerin

⇨ light corn syrup

⇨ spoon

⇨ timer

SCIENCE TAKEAWAY

Water molecules want to stick together, but detergent gets in between water molecules to separate them. When this happens, bubbles can form. Glycerin and corn syrup stick to the water molecules and make them evaporate more slowly. Slower evaporation means the bubbles take longer to pop.

1 Pinch each pipe cleaner in the middle, and bend half of it into a circle. Twist the end of the circle around the middle of the pipe cleaner to hold the circle in place. Make sure the pipe cleaner wands are all the same size.

2 Use the permanent marker and masking tape to label the cups "detergent only," "glycerin," and "corn syrup."

3 Add 1 cup of water and 2 tablespoons of liquid dishwashing soap to each cup.

4 Add an extra 1 tablespoon of water to the detergent only cup. Add 1 tablespoon of glycerin to the glycerin cup. Add 1 tablespoon of corn syrup to the corn syrup cup. Stir each cup.

5 Go outside and dip a pipe cleaner wand into the detergent only cup. Blow a bubble. Catch the bubble on your wand, and time how long the bubble lasts before it pops.

6 Catch and time at least 4 bubbles from each solution. Use a different pipe cleaner wand for each solution. Which bubbles last longest?

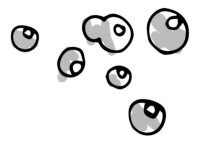

HOMEMADE COMPASS

A compass always lines up north to south.
Make your own compass so you can find your way.

🕐 **TIMEFRAME:**
   10–20 minutes

MATERIALS

⇨ strong magnet

⇨ metal sewing needle

⇨ scissors

⇨ cork

⇨ pair of pliers

⇨ small bowl

⇨ water

SCIENCE TAKEAWAY

Did you know that Earth is a giant magnet? When you rub the needle with a magnet, it becomes magnetic too. All magnets have north and south poles that push or pull each other, so Earth's magnetic poles pull the magnetic needle to point north and south.

1. Rub the magnet against the sewing needle at least 5 times. Always rub the magnet in the same direction.

2. Use the scissors to cut the cork about 0.25 inches (0.6 cm) from one of its ends, making a small cork disc that is about 0.25 inches tall.

3. Carefully use the pliers to push the needle all the way through the side of the disc. The same amount of needle should show on either side of the disc.

4. Fill a bowl with at least an inch (2.5 cm) of water.

5. Put the cork disc with the needle in the water. Try to keep the disc floating in the center of the water, away from the sides of the cup. Which way does the needle point? What happens to the needle when you turn the bowl?

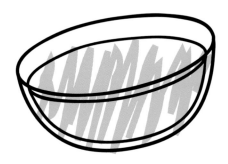

PAPER AIRPLANES

Make your own paper airplane, and find out about the forces that help a plane soar through the air.

🕐 **TIMEFRAME:** **10–20 minutes**

MATERIALS

⇨ several sheets of paper, standard size 8.5 inches x 11 inches (22 cm x 28 cm)

⇨ large open area with no wind

⇨ scissors

⇨ ruler

See folding guide on **Page 14!**

SCIENCE TAKEAWAY

Forces called thrust, lift, drag, and weight act on a paper airplane during flight. Air pushing on the plane slows it down, creating drag. When you folded the wings, this created even more drag on the airplane, causing it to slow down and not fly as far.

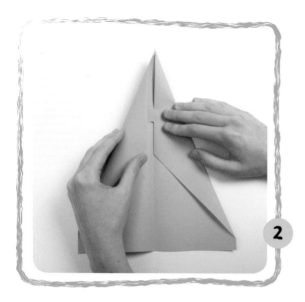

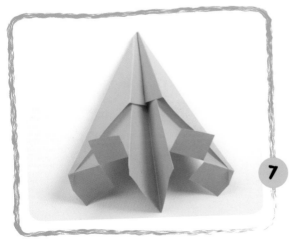

1. To make a basic dart paper airplane, fold a sheet of paper in half lengthwise. Make your fold sharp by running your thumb along the fold to crease it. Unfold the paper.

2. Fold down the top corners to meet in the middle of the paper. Then fold these creases down to meet in the middle of the paper.

3. Fold the plane in half lengthwise. Make wings by folding the edges of the paper down so they hang slightly below the centerfold.

4. Go to a large open area, and mark a starting line.

5. Place your toe at the starting line, and throw the paper plane. How far does it fly?

6. Throw the plane another 4 times, making sure the folds and points of the plane are still sharp before each throw. If your plane becomes too damaged to fly, make a new one following the instructions in steps 1 to 3. Try to throw the plane the same way each time.

7. Cut slits that are about 1 inch (2.5 cm) long where each wing meets the middle ridge, and halfway between the middle ridge and each wingtip (four slits total). Fold the inner cut sections on both wings up, and the outer cut sections down, at 90-degree angles.

8. Throw this paper plane another 5 times, just as you did before. Did anything change?

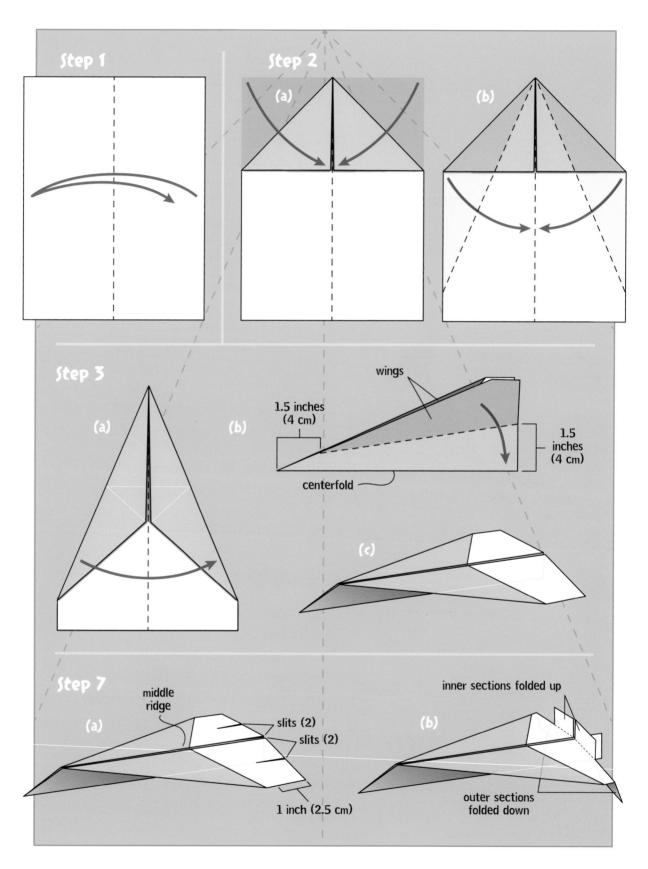

Step 1

Step 2

(a)

(b)

Step 3

(a)

(b)

wings

1.5 inches
(4 cm)

1.5 inches
(4 cm)

centerfold

(c)

Step 7

inner sections folded up

middle
ridge

(a)

slits (2)

slits (2)

(b)

outer sections
folded down

1 inch (2.5 cm)

14

KITE FLIGHT

Build your own kite, and find out how a tail changes your kite's flight.

🕐 **TIMEFRAME: 30 minutes**

MATERIALS

⇨ paper standard size
  8.5 inches x 11 inches
  (22 cm x 28 cm)

⇨ measuring tape or ruler

⇨ scissors

⇨ 2 drinking straws

⇨ tape

⇨ hole punch

⇨ kite string

⇨ paper clip

⇨ open, clear area outside
  on a windy day

⇨ plastic grocery bag

See design guide on **Page 17!**

SCIENCE TAKEAWAY

Just like with an airplane, different forces act on a kite in the air. The wind lifts the kite. The kite's weight pulls it down. A tail helps keep a kite stable by adding more weight and drag to the kite. But a tail that is too long can add too much weight and keep the kite from flying well.

1 Follow the kite guide to draw the shape of the kite on a piece of paper. Cut out your sled kite.

2 Trim the drinking straws so they will fit in the area marked for the straws. Tape the straws into place.

3 Place 3 pieces of tape on the marked areas covering the black circles. Use a hole punch to punch out the two circles.

4 Cut 2 pieces of kite string about 18 inches (45 cm) long each. Tie a string through each hole. Tie the opposite end of both strings to the same end of a paper clip.

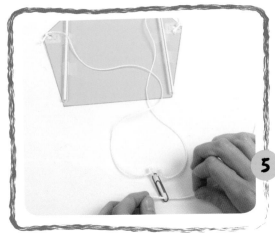

5 Cut a 40-inch (1 m) piece of kite string. Tie an end of this string to the other end of the paper clip. Your kite is ready to fly!

6 Fly your kite in an open, clear area outside. How well does it fly?

7 Lay the plastic grocery bag flat, and cut straight across the bottom of the bag to create a thin ring, about 1 inch (3 cm) wide. Cut the whole bag this way.

8 Tape a 4-inch (10 cm) strip of the grocery bag to the bottom of your kite to make a tail. Fly your kite outside again.

9 Make a tail that is 40 inches (100 cm) long by looping the grocery bag rings together. Attach the long tail to the kite. Fly your kite outside. How well does the kite fly with the longest tail compared to the other tail or no tail?

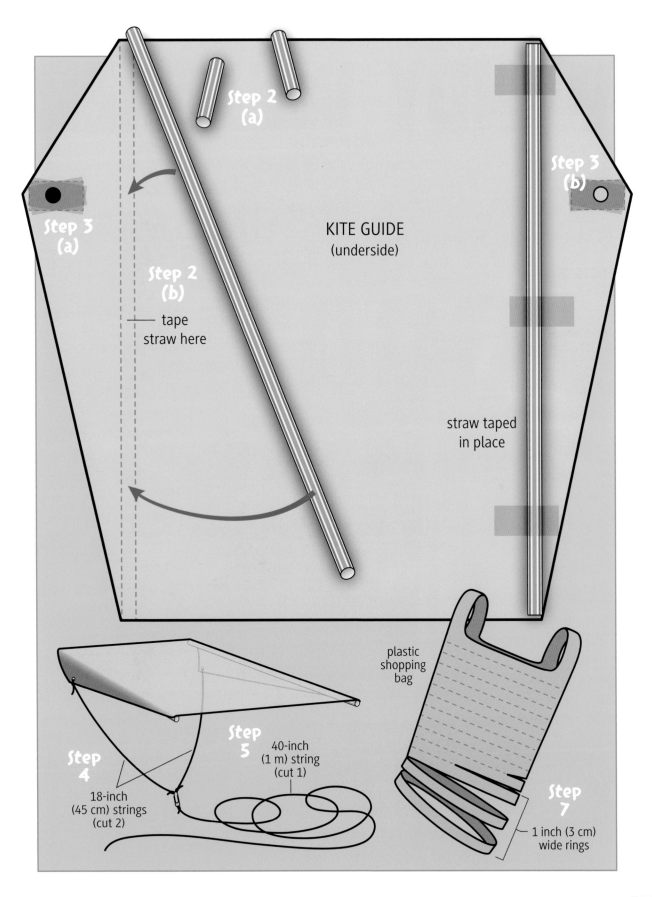

Step 2
(a)

Step 3
(b)

Step 3
(a)

KITE GUIDE
(underside)

Step 2
(b)

tape
straw here

straw taped
in place

plastic
shopping
bag

Step
4

Step
5

40-inch
(1 m) string
(cut 1)

18-inch
(45 cm) strings
(cut 2)

Step
7

1 inch (3 cm)
wide rings

WINDY WEATHER

An anemometer is a device that measures wind speed. Make your own anemometer to track the wind around your home!

🕐 **TIMEFRAME: 30 minutes**

MATERIALS

⇨ 5 (3-ounce) paper cups

⇨ paper hole punch

⇨ ruler

⇨ pencil with eraser

⇨ 2 straws

⇨ stapler

⇨ straight pin

SCIENCE TAKEAWAY

Wind forms when air moves from areas of high pressure to areas of low pressure. An anemometer catches the air as it moves. The faster the air moves, the faster the anemometer spins.

1. Punch a hole in the side of 4 cups, about 0.5 inches (1.3 cm) below the rim.

2. Punch 4 equally spaced holes around the fifth cup, about 0.25 inches (0.6 cm) below the rim. Use a pencil to poke a hole in the center of the bottom of the cup.

3. Take a single-hole cup and push about 1 inch (2.5 cm) of a straw into the cup. Staple the short end of the straw to the side of the cup. Repeat this with another single-hole cup and straw.

4. Push the long end of each straw into a side hole in the 5-hole cup and out the hole across from it.

5. Push the empty ends of each straw into the other 2 cups until about 1 inch (2.5 cm) of the straw is inside each cup. Turn all the cups to face the same direction. Staple the ends of the straws to the side of each cup.

6. Make sure all cups are about the same distance from the center of the 5-hole cup. Carefully push the pin through the 2 straws where they cross in the middle of the 5-hole cup.

7. Push the pencil through the bottom of the 5-hole cup, eraser end first, until it reaches the straws. Push the pin into the eraser.

8. The anemometer is ready to measure wind speeds. Try blowing into one of the cups or take it outside to see how the anemometer turns!

HEAVY HULA

Who knew there was science in spinning a hoop around your body? Will a heavy or a light hoop spin better?

🕐 **TIMEFRAME: 30 minutes**

MATERIALS

⇨ tape measure

⇨ poly pipe, polyethylene pipe, or plastic pipe, 1 inch (2.5 cm) diameter, about 25 feet (7.6 m) long

⇨ PVC cutter or a sharp utility knife

⇨ poly insert coupling or wooden dowel that fits snugly inside the poly pipe tubing

⇨ hair dryer

⇨ duct tape

⇨ funnel with an opening that can fit into the poly pipe

⇨ measuring cup

⇨ sand

⇨ timer

SCIENCE TAKEAWAY

You need to spin a hoop fast enough to prevent it from falling. As you spin it, your hips push it up. You will have to work harder to spin a heavier hoop, and it will be harder to stop it from falling.

1. Measure the height from the ground to somewhere between the belly button and the middle of the chest of the person who will spin the hoop. This will be the diameter of the hoop.

2. Multiply that number by 3.14. You'll need this length of pipe to make a hoop.

3. Measure the length of pipe needed, and ask an adult to cut the tubing to the right size with a PVC cutter.

4. Use a poly insert coupling or wooden dowel to connect the ends of the tubing so they form a circle. Insert the coupling about halfway into one end of the tubing. Then insert the other half of the coupling into the tubing's other end. Push the tubing together until no coupling is visible. Use the hair dryer to warm the tubing if it is difficult to insert the coupling.

5. Put a short strip of duct tape over the connection where the ends of tubing meet.

6. Make a second hoop the same size. This time, use a funnel to pour 1 cup of sand into the tubing before connecting the ends.

7. Have someone spin the lighter hoop around his or her hips. Time this for 30 seconds, and count how many full turns the hoop makes.

8. Repeat step 7 with the heavier hoop. What's the difference between the two hoops?

21

BAKING SODA ROCKET

Use simple ingredients to launch a rocket (almost) into space!

🕐 **TIMEFRAME: 20-30 minutes**

MATERIALS

⇨ measuring spoons

⇨ baking soda

⇨ bowl

⇨ water

⇨ spoon

⇨ plastic film canister with a lid and tight seal

⇨ vinegar

⇨ open outdoor area

⇨ safety goggles

⇨ paper towel

SCIENCE TAKEAWAY

When vinegar and baking soda mix, carbon dioxide gas forms. The pressure of the gas builds up inside the canister, causing the canister to pop open and launch into the air. The more carbon dioxide, the higher the launch.

1. Place 1 teaspoon of baking soda into the bowl. Add $\frac{1}{8}$ teaspoon of water to the baking soda and mix.

2. Pack the inside of the canister lid with the damp baking soda. Do not put baking soda where the canister snaps onto the lid. The baking soda should stay in place. If it falls out, add more water.

3. Add 3 teaspoons of vinegar to the canister.

4. Go outside to an open area at least 10 feet (3 m) from buildings.

5. Put on your safety goggles. Stoop down near the ground, and quickly snap the lid onto the canister to seal it. Immediately, turn the canister over, so the lid is on the ground. Quickly move away and wait for the reaction to occur. The cap should separate and the canister should launch into the air. If the rocket did not launch, you may not have sealed the lid tightly or quickly enough.

6. Rinse and dry the lid and canister.

7. Repeat steps 1-5, this time using 5 teaspoons of vinegar. How high does the canister go compared to the previous launch?

BUG VACUUM

Have you ever noticed how many tiny creatures live all around you?
Make this bug vacuum to learn about the insects living in your backyard.

🕐 **TIMEFRAME: 30 minutes**

MATERIALS

⇨ hole punch or leather awl

⇨ plastic container with a lid

⇨ ruler

⇨ 2 flexible drinking straws

⇨ tape

⇨ pen or pencil

⇨ nylon stocking

⇨ scissors

⇨ clear plastic wrap

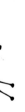

SCIENCE TAKEAWAY

Having many types of plants and animals living in an area is called biodiversity.
The more biodiversity, the healthier an area is. How healthy is the area around
your home?

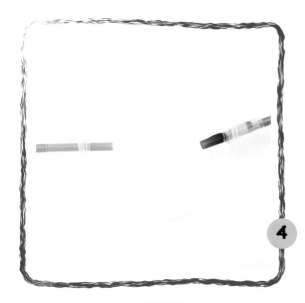

1. With an adult's help, use a hole punch or a leather awl to make a hole on both sides of the plastic container, about 0.4 inches (1 cm) below the top rim of the container. The container's lid should not block the holes.

2. Insert the mouth end of a flexible straw into one of the holes. Make sure the straw fits tightly into the hole by wrapping tape around it or making the hole wider using a pen or pencil.

3. Cover the mouth end of the other straw with a piece of nylon stocking. Tape the stocking to the straw.

4. Insert the mouth of the covered flexible straw into the other hole in the plastic container. Make sure it fits tightly.

5. Use scissors to cut out the center of the plastic container's lid, leaving a 0.4-inch (1 cm) border around the rim of the lid.

6. Stretch a piece of clear plastic wrap over the top of the plastic container and snap the lid back on to hold the plastic wrap in place.

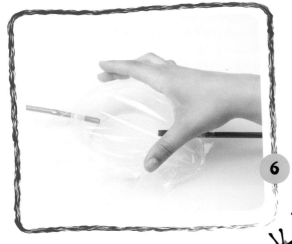

7. Take your bug vacuum outside to collect insects. When you find a bug, gently place the end of the open straw very close to the insect. Place the straw with the nylon filter in your mouth, and breathe in to suck the insect into the container.

8. Examine the insects you collected through the window of the insect vacuum. How many different types of insects did you collect? When you have finished, release them near where you caught them.

TAKE THE TEMPERATURE

Have you ever wondered how thermometers work? Make your own liquid-filled thermometer to find out.

🕐 **TIMEFRAME: 30 minutes**

MATERIALS

⇨ narrow-necked, small, plastic bottle with lid (vanilla extract bottles work well)

⇨ rubbing alcohol

⇨ liquid food coloring

⇨ medicine dropper or syringe

⇨ modeling clay

⇨ clear plastic drinking straw that fits into the mouth of the bottle

⇨ permanent marker

⇨ warm water

⇨ small bowl

⇨ cold water

SCIENCE TAKEAWAY

Most materials expand when they get warmer and contract when they become cooler. When the liquid in a thermometer gets warm, it takes up more space, so the fluid level in the thermometer rises. When the liquid cools, it takes up less space, and the level in the thermometer goes down.

1. Empty and wash the plastic bottle. Fill it about halfway with rubbing alcohol.

2. Add a couple of drops of food coloring to the alcohol, close the bottle, and shake it so the liquids mix well.

3. Fill a medicine dropper or syringe with the colored rubbing alcohol, and set it aside. Make sure the bottle is still between a quarter and halfway full of rubbing alcohol.

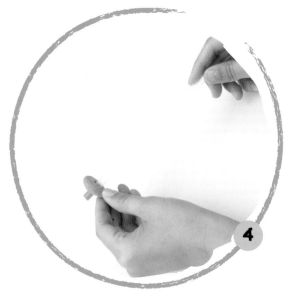

4 Mold the modeling clay until it feels soft. Then form a ball and push it flat. This piece of clay should be bigger than the neck of your bottle. Use your straw to punch a hole in the middle of the clay, just big enough to allow the straw to go through. Remove any clay clogging the straw. Poke the straw through the hole in your modeling clay. Place the clay on the bottle's neck so the straw hangs into the liquid but does not touch the bottom of the bottle. Most of the straw will be sticking out of the bottle.

5 Use the modeling clay to seal the bottle opening and to hold the straw in place. Make sure the clay forms a tight seal around the straw and over the bottle mouth.

6 Drip the contents of your medicine dropper or syringe into the straw. The fluid should rise up the straw and stay there. If it runs into the bottle, the clay is not sealing the bottle.

7 The fluid level should reach about midway up the visible part of the straw. If needed, use the dropper or syringe to add more alcohol to the straw.

8 Observe the fluid level in the straw. This level indicates room temperature. Use the permanent marker to make a small line to indicate this fluid level on your straw.

9 Put some warm water in a small bowl, and place your bottle in the water. Give the thermometer a little time to work. Does the fluid level in the straw change?

10 Fill the bowl with cold water. Place your bottle in the water, and let the thermometer adjust to the new temperature. What happens?

MORE TO EXPLORE

Who knew you could do so much science in your backyard? What did you learn? What questions do you have? What do you still want to find out?

What do you think would happen if you made your paper airplane bigger or cut your kite into a different shape? Do you think there's an area near your home that has more biodiversity than your yard does? Go ahead and find out!

For even more outdoor projects, scan this QR code!

GLOSSARY

biodiversity: the existence of many different kinds of plants and animals in an environment

contract: to become smaller

diameter: the distance through the center of an object from one side to the other

drag: a push or pull that opposes the motion of an object moving through air or liquid

evaporate: to change from liquid into gas

expand: to grow larger

force: a push or pull that acts on an object

lift: the upward force that acts on a flying object

molecule: the smallest piece a material can be divided into without changing how it behaves

pressure: the push of gas or liquid molecules against a surface

thrust: the forward force on a flying object. When you throw a paper airplane, you give the plane thrust.

FURTHER INFORMATION

For more information and projects, visit **Science Buddies** at **https://www.sciencebuddies.org/**.

Heinecke, Liz Lee. *Outdoor Science Lab for Kids: 52 Family-Friendly Experiments for the Yard, Garden, Playground, and Park*. Beverly, MA: Quarry Books, 2016.

Ives, Rob. *Build Your Own Rockets and Planes*. Minneapolis: Hungry Tomato, 2018.

Ives, Rob. *Fun Experiments with Forces and Motion: Hovercrafts, Rockets, and More*. Minneapolis: Hungry Tomato, 2018.

INDEX

airplane, 12–14, 30

anemometer, 18–19

biodiversity, 24, 30

bubbles, 4, 8–9

carbon dioxide, 22

compass, 10–11

drag, 12, 15

force, 12, 15

kite, 15–17, 30

magnet, 10–11

materials, 6, 8, 10, 12, 15, 18, 20, 22, 24, 26

pressure, 18, 22

rocket, 4, 22–23

safety, 7, 22–23

thermometer, 26–29

weight, 12, 15

wind, 4, 12, 15, 18–19

PHOTO ACKNOWLEDGMENTS

The images in this book are used with the permission of: Design element (pencil) © primiaou/Shutterstock Images, pp. 8, 10, 12, 15, 18, 20, 22, 24, 26; © Visual Generation/Shutterstock Images, pp. 1 (clock), 30 (clock); © Mighty Media, Inc., pp. 1 (thermometer), 7 (ruler, string, hair dryer, utility knife, hole punch, scissors), 8–29 (project photos), 15 (kite), 18 (anemometer), 20 (hula hoop), 27 (thermometer), 29 (thermometer); © Artur Balytskyi/Shutterstock Images, pp. 1 (compass), 10 (compass); © Tom and Kwikki/Shutterstock Images, pp. 1 (bubbles), 8 (bubbles), 9 (bubbles); © primiaou/Shutterstock Images, pp. 1 (rocket), 22 (rocket); © Tiwat K/Shutterstock Images, pp. 3 (paper airplanes), 12 (paper airplanes), 31 (computer); © Ermak Oksana/Shutterstock Images, pp. 3 (bugs), 24 (bugs), 25 (bugs); © Denis Pogostin/Shutterstock Images, p. 4 (girl throwing airplane); © Rawpixel.com/Shutterstock Images, pp. 5 (children hula hooping), 6 (boy with recycling); © Gavran333/Shutterstock Images, p. 7 (goggles); © Minur/Shutterstock Images, p. 11 (bowl of water); Laura Westlund/Independent Picture Service, pp. 14, 17 (illustrations); © Sudowoodo/Shutterstock Images, p. 27 (sun); © Nina Puankova/Shutterstock Images, p. 29 (snowflakes)

Front cover: © mhatzapa/Shutterstock Images (kite, leaf); © Mighty Media, Inc. (paper airplane); © primiaou/Shutterstock Images (magnet); © STILLFX/Shutterstock Images (background); © Visual Generation/Shutterstock Images (clock)

Back cover: © Artur Balytskyi/Shutterstock Images (butterfly); © primiaou/Shutterstock Images (pencil); © STILLFX/Shutterstock Images (background); © Sudowoodo/Shutterstock Images (sun); © Tom and Kwikki/Shutterstock Images (magnifying glass, molecules)